IRAN
AND
IRAQ

NATIONS
AT
WAR

IRAN AND IRAQ

LISA MANNETTI

FRANKLIN WATTS 1986 AN IMPACT BOOK
NEW YORK LONDON TORONTO SYDNEY

A GROLIER COMPANY

Map by Vantage Art, Inc.

Photographs courtesy of:
AP/Wide World: pp. 4, 6, 13, 27, 30, 34,
49, 60, 70, 76; UPI/Bettmann Newsphotos:
pp. 7, 9, 10, 40, 52; Rob Walls/Black Star:
p. 18; Islamic Republic of Iran, War
Information Headquarters: pp. 28, 33, 35,
36, 43, 44, 45, 46, 63, 64, 74;
Manoocher/Black Star: p. 31.

Library of Congress Cataloging-in-Publication Data
Mannetti, Lisa.
Iran and Iraq : nations at war.
(An Impact book)
Bibliography: p.
Includes index.
Summary: Surveys the historical background and
recent events of the war between Iran and Iraq and
considers the resulting political and economic
complications for the region and for oil-dependent
countries.
1. Iraqi-Iranian Conflict, 1980-   —Juvenile
literature. [1. Iraqui-Iranian Conflict, 1980-   ]
I. Title.
DS318.85.M36 1986   955'.054   85-26516
ISBN 0-531-10155-X

CONTENTS

IRAN
AND
IRAQ

CHAPTER
ONE
AN INTRODUCTION

The Iran-Iraq war involves complex issues that are entangled in historical, cultural, and religious disputes. In a very real sense, the two nations have been squabbling over the same issues for hundreds of years. Battles fought in the seventh century are invoked as war cries in the modern conflict. A disagreement between two religious sects that began hundreds of years ago still raises fears of rebellion throughout the Persian Gulf.

To complicate matters, experts cannot agree about which nation began the conflict—although the blame is generally placed on Iraq. Nor does anyone know the *real* reason for the war. We do know, however, that a series of intertwined events both directly and indirectly led to the war that has continued for nearly five years. These circumstances include the Iranian revolution, Iraq's desire for a position of political influence in the Gulf, Iraq's fears of Shi'a revolution, its desire to regain control of an important waterway between the two countries, and its perception of Iran as a weak and disorganized neighbor that could easily be vanquished.

Although the war has so far been confined to Iran and Iraq, the possibility of regional and worldwide involvement always exists, If the scope of the war were to widen, the

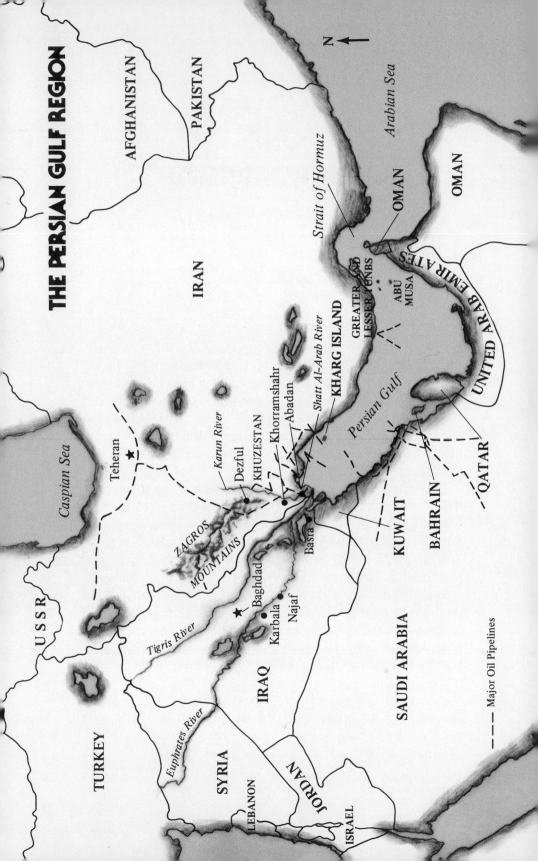

results could be disastrous. The West is dependent on the Gulf region for oil; in fact, the area is said to be of "vital interest" to the United States. The Gulf nations, on the other hand, are afraid that the superpowers might interfere in the conflict. If that happened, these small countries would be caught in the middle of the rivalry between the Soviet Union and the United States.

IRAN

Iran, which was called Persia until 1935, is a large country —more than twice as big as Texas. It is bounded on the north by the Soviet Union and the Caspian Sea and on the east by Afghanistan and Pakistan. To the south lies the Persian Gulf. Iraq shares its western border for 780 miles (1248 km).

In 1953, with the help of the United States, the Iranian government was overthrown and Shah Mohammed Reza Pahlavi was restored to the throne. For more than twenty years, Iran underwent rapid economic growth. Under the Shah's direction, money from oil revenues was used to develop Iran. Dams, roads, ports, and railroads were built. Industries were created where none had previously existed. But rapid spending brought high inflation. As a result, by the mid-1970s the purchase of a house or even a car was beyond the means of a middle-class family.

The Shah led Iran into the twentieth century but at a cost. He created a rigid atmosphere of repression—the press was heavily censored, Parliament was his "rubber stamp," and only one political party was allowed during his one-man rule. The Shah also commanded a large secret police force known as SAVAK. Almost four thousand SAVAK agents regularly hunted down those who opposed the Shah.

From 1978 onward, civil unrest was common in Iran. There were demonstrations and riots. Shi'a religious leaders began organizing protests over the whole country. As time went on, these protests became more radical. The Shah, in

Shah Mohammed Reza Pahlavi in full regalia,
seated on the Peacock Throne, 1971

an effort to quiet the rising tide of dissent, became more autocratic. As a result, those who had been moderate in their demands for reform became increasingly radical. In the fall of 1978, strikes against the oil industry, the post office, government factories, and banks demolished the economy.

The Shah tried to make concessions, but it was already too late. In January 1979, he fled the country. Shapur Bakhtiar, the prime minister, tried to save the faltering government. He disbanded SAVAK and granted freedom of the press. But one million Iranians marched in Teheran, the capital, demanding Bakhtiar's resignation. On February 1, 1979, the Ayatollah Ruhollah Khomeini returned to Iran from nearly fifteen years of exile and the revolutionary government took over.

THE REVOLUTIONARY GOVERNMENT IN IRAN

The takeover by the revolutionary government drastically changed the political, social, and economic institutions of Iran. The nation was no longer a monarchy but a republic. Control of the economy shifted from the private sector to the government. But most important, the nation ceased to be a secular state and became a theocracy—a country ruled by religious leaders—as the Shi'as (also known as Shi'ites) assumed power.

Khomeini, the leader of the revolution, had been exiled to Iraq, but in October of 1978, he was asked to leave that country and went to Paris. From Paris it was actually easier to foment rebellion in Iran. He had better communications with the leaders of the revolution, he was given press coverage, and he worked hard to undermine the power of the Shah. At the same time, Shi'a religious leaders were stirring up Iranian citizens with propaganda and rallying converts to their cause by harping on religious concepts such as

Above: *after the Shah's departure from Iran, Teheran, the capital city, became a battleground. Troops loyal to the Shah and troops in support of the Ayatollah Khomeini waged a struggle for control of the government.* Left: *the Islamic leader, the Ayatollah Ruhollah Khomeini returned to Iran from exile in 1979. He established an Islamic republic in Iran.*

shahadat (martyrdom) and *sultane zalem* (moral indignation against a corrupt ruler).

Anti-American sentiment was strong. The United States had permitted the Shah to remain in New York for treatment of cancer. This caused such outrage that a group of Iranian revolutionaries who called themselves "students following the Imam's (an imam is a leader; the name applied to Khomeini) line" seized the U.S. embassy in Teheran on November 4, 1979, taking fifty-four Americans hostage. In April 1980, the United States attempted to rescue the hostages. But two helicopters failed; then a third helicopter and a C-130 airplane crashed. Eight Americans were killed in the blaze that followed. Many Iranians believed the failure of the rescue mission was a miracle. They thought God had intervened to save their revolution. The hostages were released on January 21, 1981, after being held for more than a year.

OPPOSITION TO
KHOMEINI'S REGIME

The Ayatollah Khomeini had called many of the Shah's actions "inhuman." Yet his regime has been equally harsh. When an Islamic judge had hundreds of people executed on very slim evidence, Khomeini said nothing. Many people were condemned for crimes involving drugs or sex, which were regarded as "corruption of the earth." These people were often executed in public in a grisly manner. Many were killed by firing squads; some were hanged; others were buried up to the chest and then pelted with stones.

Many Iranians, glad to see the end of the Shah's regime, also opposed the revolutionary regime. Some became active in leftist radical groups. One guerrilla group, the Mojahedin, may have been responsible for an attempt to violently overthrow the Khomeini government. In a series of bombings between June and August 1981, they assassinated the secretary general of Iran, several members of Parliament

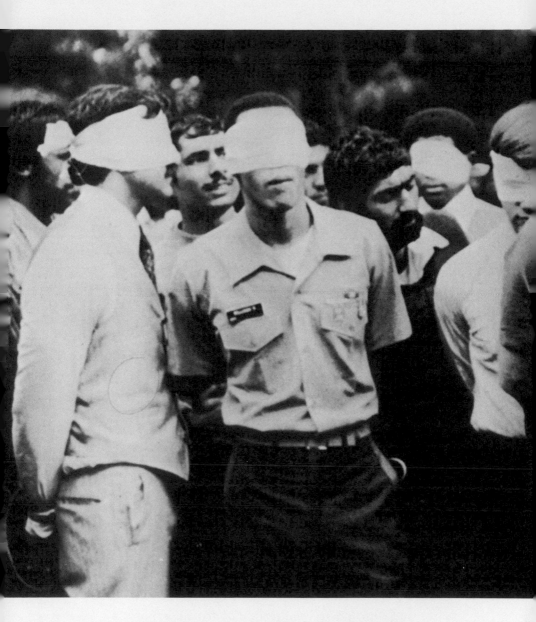

American hostages seized by militant Iranians
in Teheran in 1979 are shown
being paraded by their captors.

Kurdish rebels and former police officers of the Shah being executed by a firing squad after a brief trial. Once in power, Khomeini showed no tolerance for opponents.

and cabinet ministers, the national chief of police, the chief justice, the prime minister, and the president. They also killed a number of Islamic prayer leaders in major cities.

Khomeini took steps to quash the anti-revolutionary forces. One account estimates that 8,000 Mojahedin were killed between June 1981 and September 1983. About 85 percent of them were executed, and the rest died in street battles or by torture. Some 50 percent of the Mojahedin killed were high school or college students. The executions, far from being kept secret, were conducted openly in order to frighten people and dissuade them from joining the counterrevolution. In one instance, four high school teachers were shot in the schoolyard in front of their students.

KHOMEINI'S POWER

Despite the turmoil, Khomeini has managed to retain power in Iran by shrewdly manipulating the press, the economy, and the military.

He makes certain that the government completely controls the media. All newspapers, television broadcasts, and radio programs are under strict control. He does this because he knows that government propaganda helps sway the masses. Two important propaganda themes are praise of the revolution and of Islam, and hatred of the United States. For example, the government spread the rumor that the Mojahedin were American agents. It also sent out the message that many executions of enemies of the state were justified in the name of religion even though many Islamic scholars do not condone the ayatollah's actions.

Khomeini also controls the treasury and the flow of money to other religious leaders. Those who disagree with him face severe economic retribution.

Furthermore, he has at his disposal the Revolutionary Guards, or Pasdaran. He has used them ruthlessly to crush the counterrevolutionaries and to wage war against Iraq. Most of these guards came from the poorer classes. Khomeini helped them rise above poverty and appointed many of them to high-level government posts. As a result, the Pasdaran are fiercely loyal to the ayatollah.

Some experts believe the revolution in Iran was the most significant cause of the war between the two countries. The revolutionaries' attempt to topple the government raised fears throughout the Gulf, but especially in Iraq. In addition, some analysts note that President Hussein of Iraq probably believed that the turmoil in Iran meant it was weak and would be easy to defeat. Perhaps Hussein also believed that the United States would not support the Khomeini regime because of the hostage crisis.

Many observers wonder what will happen to Iran after Khomeini dies. Will the war and the revolution continue? Some say the answer may depend on whether Khomeini grooms a successor during his lifetime. Still, no one can be certain what the fate of Iran is likely to be when Khomeini's rule comes to an end.

IRAQ

Oil-rich Iraq, once known as Mesopotamia, has a population of 14 million. It is surrounded by Turkey on the north, Saudi Arabia and Kuwait on the south, Iran on the east, and Syria and Jordan on the west.

In 1957 Saddam Hussein, before he was president, joined the underground Ba'ath party, a socialist group that opposed Western culture. The Ba'ath party does not identify itself with religion, but with solidarity among those who speak Arabic. In addition, the Ba'ath party is strongly anti-imperialist and anti-Zionist.

In 1959 Hussein attempted to assassinate Iraq's leader. He escaped, but was ultimately captured and imprisoned for two years. When the Ba'ath party came to power in Iraq in 1968, he became the deputy secretary. In 1979 he

Iraq's President Saddam Hussein

made himself president of Iraq and has carefully guarded his position since then. It is estimated that President Hussein had some 250 of his opponents executed between 1978 and 1980.

Under Hussein's leadership, the economy of Iraq has vastly improved. Salaries are higher, education is free, and medical care and facilities are more modern. Shops sell a variety of imported clothes and goods.

As the war with Iran has continued, a personality cult has developed around President Hussein. His picture is displayed everywhere around the country. He has been called the Knight of Iraq and the Sword of the Arabs.

Interestingly, in both Iran and Iraq the leaders are regarded as heroes. Khomeini is likened to Imam Hussein, the prophet Mohammed's grandson who fled Mecca in the eighth century and returned to conquer a tyrant. But despite their similarities, Iran and Iraq criticize each other constantly. The people of Iran have compared Hussein to Satan. They call him an enemy of Islam and humanity. In turn, the Iraqis refer to Khomeini as a senile old charlatan.

While propaganda is broadcast to inspire the residents, both governments are extremely secretive. A likely reason is the closeness of the war and the need to maintain tight security. In Iraq, for example, telephone directories are not given out. Maps that are too well defined cannot be sold. Diplomats must secure permits to travel beyond the confines of the capital, Baghdad.

Finally, both countries have much at stake in the war. Their economies have been devastated; thousands of people have died; cities and towns have been destroyed—and there is no end in sight.

CHAPTER
TWO
HISTORICAL
AND
RELIGIOUS
BACKGROUNDS

In A.D. 637 the Arabs defeated the Persians (Iranians) at the Battle of Qadissiyaa. Although it would seem a seventh-century battle would have little impact on modern Iraq and Iran, references to the Arab victory are common. In fact, the war is often called Saddam's [Hussein's] Qadissiyaa. This is but one indication of age-old religious and cultural hostility between the two nations.

In another ancient religious dispute several centuries ago, a split occurred between two Islamic sects: the Sunnis and the Shi'as. The Sunnis accepted the best-qualified man in the tribe as caliph, the temporal and spiritual head of Islam. The Shi'as insisted only a direct descendant of Mohammed could serve as caliph.

Hostility between Sunnis and Shi'as has persisted to this day. Sunni Arabs have been able to control nearly every Muslim government. In fact, Sunnis, who made up one-half of Iraq's population, control its politics. In contrast, Shi'as —or Shi'ites—have had little political success, although Shi'ism was adopted by Iran (at that time Persia) as the official state religion in the sixteenth century.

Shi'ites make up the other half of the total population of Iraq. Most of them are poor and live in the south. Ironically,

Shi'ism's holiest shrines are located not in Iran but in Iraq, in the towns of Karbala and An Najaf.

PAN-ISLAMISM— EXPORTING THE REVOLUTION

When the Ayatollah Khomeini (a Shi'ite Muslim) came to power in Iran in 1979 many Muslim governments feared that revolution would erupt in their countries, too. Some analysts believe it was Iraq's fear of internal Shi'a rebellion that brought about the war with Iran.

Indeed, Ruhollah Khomeini called on the Shi'ites of Iraq to revolt against their government. He publicly denounced President Hussein and the Ba'ath party. He branded Hussein an infidel (a person who is not a Muslim) and accused him of being "pro-Western"—a terrible insult in anti-American Iran. Khomeini declared: "The Islamic government cannot sit at the peace table with a government that has no faith in Islam and humanity. Islam does not allow peace between a Muslim and an infidel."

The Iranian constitution gives legal status to Pan-Islamism. The goal of Pan-Islamism is political harmony and unity among all Muslims. It calls on Muslims not to fight one another and to follow a single leader. Therefore, exporting the revolution is both a Pan-Islamic and Iranian goal, and a mandate of the constitution. Both Pan-Arabism and Pan-Islamism urge people to unite, but they have different secular and religious goals. Some experts say that part of the current conflict is a clash between Pan-Arabist and Pan-Islamic goals.

President Saddam Hussein of Iraq responded to fears of Shi'ite rebellion by banishing thousands of Iraqis of Persian heritage. The Ayatollah Muhammed al-Baqr al-Sadr had such a large following that he was called the Khomeini of Iraq. Hussein took no chances and had the ayatollah executed. At the same time, Hussein tried to appease the

Iraqi Shi'ite population by improving their standard of living.

Still, Khomeini's magnetic personal appeal to millions, his link to the Shi'ites in Iraq, his calls for the destruction of Hussein and the Ba'ath party, and his encouragement of violence have led many people to believe that the religious conflict is one of the principal causes of the war. Others say that religion is just one cause of the animosity between the two nations, but not the main issue.

THE KURDS

The Kurds of Iran, Iraq, and Turkey are members of many different tribes who are united by a common language and culture. They are the largest minority group in Iran, numbering several million.

The Kurdish language is related to Persian. For that reason, the Shah frequently referred to the "Persian-Kurdish Brotherhood." His references did not win over many Kurds, however, as they rarely benefited from Iran's rapid economic development.

In the 1970s, the Kurds of Iraq rebelled against the government in an effort to gain independence. The Shah of Iran received U.S. aid with which to help the Kurds. The CIA also gave assistance. The Shah set up Iranian Kurdistan as a receiving point for arms and weapons to the Kurds and as a refuge for Iraqi Kurdish rebels.

Iraq was unable to put down the Kurdish uprising. In exchange for an end to Iranian aid to Iraqi Kurdish rebels, Iraq agreed to sign the 1975 Algiers Treaty between the two nations. The chief negotiator for Iraq was President Saddam Hussein. But Hussein felt he was pressured to sign. He made concessions only in the hope of ending Iran's support of the rebels.

Some analysts of the current Iran-Iraq crisis consider Hussein's dilemma a significant cause of the war. He was forced to agree to the terms of the Algiers Treaty to bring

a halt to a costly rebellion. As a result, Hussein felt humiliated, these experts feel, and wanted to regain the position Iraq had lost under the agreement. His desire for vengeance was another cause of the war, the experts say.

Kurdish guerrillas.
The Kurds have been fighting
for self-rule for centuries.

CHAPTER THREE

GEOPOLITICS: THE SHATT-AL-ARAB AND OTHER DISPUTES

The Shatt-al-Arab is a river that runs for several miles along the border between Iran and Iraq. It is 127 miles (203 km) long and is formed by the confluence of the Tigris and Euphrates rivers. Despite its tranquil beauty, it has been the cause of disputes since the sixteenth century. The extreme importance of the waterway to both countries has led many observers to believe it is one of the most important causes of the war between Iran and Iraq. Indeed, both nations have historical, legal, and geographic reasons to support their claims to the Shatt.

THE SECOND ERZERUM TREATY, 1847

A cycle of warfare, numerous peace treaties, and more warfare occurred in the eighteenth and nineteenth centuries. The Ottomans and the Persians were again on the brink of war when Great Britain and Russia offered to negotiate a peaceful solution. In 1843 delegates from all four nations met for the first time, but it took four years of angry debate and conflict to produce the Treaty of 1847. Among other provisions, the Shatt-al-Arab was awarded to the Ottomans (who ruled Iraq) up to the deep-water marker on the eastern shore. And the 1847 treaty gave anchorage rights to the Persians (Iranians) at Khorramshahr in the Karun River (which is in Iran) just *above* the Shatt, and not *in* the Shatt. Both the Ottomans and the Persians had free use of the entire river, but further problems and arguments arose. According to the treaty, a boundary commission with delegates from Great Britain, Russia, Persia, and the Ottoman Empire was to be established. But the committee clashed over the interpretation of this part of the treaty. The Persian delegate argued that the treaty granted his nation the entire territory east of the Shatt; the Ottoman commissioner was equally steadfast and maintained that the issue had been left unresolved. In the end, twenty years passed before a map was drawn that all four nations agreed upon.

THE CONSTANTINOPLE PROTOCOL OF 1913

In 1911, the Ottomans and the Persians once again attempted to establish clear boundaries. After eighteen meetings, however, they were still arguing. Once again, Britain and Russia intervened, and in 1913 all four countries signed the Constantinople Protocol and agreed to set up a new boundary commission. According to the Protocol, most —but not all—of the Shatt belonged to the Ottomans. The boundary committee set out to define the line of demarcation. But just at that time, World War I broke out. The Ottoman Empire joined the war on the side of Germany and never ratified the Protocol of 1913.

THE TREATY OF 1937

After World War I, Iran and Iraq entered a short era known as the Independent Period. In 1920 Iraq became a mandate under British administration. It was declared a kingdom one year later, in 1921. In 1924 the Ottoman Empire was abolished. In 1925 Iran was under the rule of Reza Shah who became increasingly angry over Iraq's complete dominance of the Shatt. As both countries began building ports, oil facilities, and roads in the area, the Shatt took on a new importance.

In the first few years of Iraq's independence, Iran did not recognize the new state. Then, in 1929, it granted recognition to Iraq most likely because Britain had gained much power in the Middle East. The shah hoped that the oil interests Britain shared in Iran would convince the British to make concessions regarding the Shatt. Iran wanted half the river, which neither the British nor the Iraqis would give up.

As time went on it seemed to Iraq that Iran was continually ignoring the boundary agreement. Therefore, Iraq complained to the League of Nations in 1934. The Iraqis also objected that the 1847 Treaty left them with only one harbor, Basra, on the Persian Gulf.

Perhaps both countries began to realize that the earlier treaties, which had regarded the river as a natural boundary, were no longer advantageous as oil shipping made the waterway vital to each.

Iran retorted that the 1913 Protocol was invalid because the Ottomans had never ratified it. In any case, Iran argued further, the Russians had forced the Iranians to sign it. However, international law does not recognize duress as a reason to cancel an agreement.

When a coup brought about a change in the government of Iraq, the new leaders made a peaceful settlement with Iran. In 1937 the two nations signed a treaty that established the same conditions as the Protocol of 1913, but altered the border in one instance: for five miles around Abadan, a crucial port for Iran, the boundary followed the *thalweg*, the midline or deepest part of a river.

THE 1975 ALGIERS TREATY

The cycle of dispute, treaty, and discord continued for the next thirty years. In 1969, Iraq claimed the entire river. Both Iran and Iraq insisted they had signed the previous accord only because of British pressure. Offensives and retaliatory acts followed. Iraq deported some 70,000 Iranians who lived in the Shi'a shrine cities. Iran gave massive support to the Kurdish rebels waging civil war in Iraq. The Shah let it be known he would continue to back the Kurds until Iraq gave up its control over the Shatt.

Finally in 1975, the Algiers Agreement was reached. Faced with the devastating effects of the Kurdish uprising, Iraq gave up half the Shatt-al-Arab to Iran. The new boundary was set along the *thalweg*.

In the setting of the present war, many experts believe that Iraq was smarting from the terms of the 1975 treaty, and so, waited patiently in the gathering shadows until it perceived Iran was weak. On September 17, 1980, Saddam Hussein of Iraq declared the Shatt was "totally Iraqi and totally Arab."

The Shatt is vital to both countries. The centuries-old disputes have infused the issue with emotion and a sense of national pride. The end result has been a war that has continued for nearly five years.

KHUZESTAN, ABU MUSA, AND THE GREATER AND LESSER TUNBS

The territory of Khuzestan, which borders the Shatt, was under Ottoman rule until 1924 when it came under Iranian control. (It was formerly called Arabistan.) Eighty percent of the people of Khuzestan speak Arabic even though it is part of non-Arab Iran. If Iraq were able to annex this large territory, it would add enormously to its prestige in the Persian Gulf. In addition, vast oil reserves are located in

Khuzestan. Conquering it would add to the Iraqi oil supply and lessen Iran's oil wealth.

In 1971, under the Shah's regime, Iran had seized Abu Musa, Greater Tunb, and Lesser Tunb. These are three small uninhabited islands in the Persian Gulf. They had belonged to the United Arab Emirates (UAE). But the Shah declared Iran had to take them over in order to ensure the safe passage of ships. The Arab states were angered by the Shah's arrogance and deceptive reasoning, but they took no action. Naturally, Iraq also wanted control over the islands. When Khomeini assumed power, he refused to give up the islands, because he was certain Iraq would hand them over to the United States.

Both Iran and Iraq recognize the strategic value of the islands because they lie close to the Strait of Hormuz— "the oil jugular of the West." All ships must pass through the strait to enter or leave the Persian Gulf.

Khuzestan and the islands of Abu Musa, Greater Tunb, and Lesser Tunb are important to both Iran and Iraq. But the conflict over the Shatt-al-Arab was probably the most important cause of the war. The long years of discord over control of the river, the national feelings it arouses, the necessity of the Shatt to both nations—all these realities have resulted in a state of warfare. But ironically, the tug-of-war has led to an impasse. At present, neither nation can use the river. Iran's Abadan facility has been destroyed, and Iraq must export its oil by overland pipeline.

CHAPTER
FOUR
THE OUTBREAK
OF WAR

In September 1980, Iraq claimed Iran attacked Khanaqin. Fighting and skirmishes broke out along the border and along the Shatt-al-Arab. In September Saddam Hussein renounced the 1975 Algiers Treaty in these words: "This Shatt shall again be, as it has throughout history, Iraqi and Arab in name and in reality, with all rights of full sovereignty over it." Most people believe Iraq started the war. Five days after President Hussein abrogated the treaty, Iraq attacked ten Iranian airfields. Iraq apparently decided to go to war when it thought Iran was weak. Iran was beset by political turmoil, rebellion, and economic troubles. Furthermore, there was little chance a superpower—notably the United States—would come to Iran's aid. Despite their former ties, Iran and the United States were bitter enemies because of the hostage situation. Finally, Iraq wanted to gain power in the Gulf, and it expected to win the war against Iran quickly and easily. But the fighting has continued for nearly five years, and experts do not expect it to end in the near future.

Early in the war, Iraq hinted that it would not attack oil installations. Iran responded by attacking Iraqi oil facilities. Within a matter of days, major oil installations in both countries had been severely damaged.

Iraqi forces then moved into Iran's oil-rich province of Khuzestan. After a month of heavy fighting in the streets, the city of Khorramshahr (meaning Greenness and Happiness) fell into Iraqi hands. The fighting had been extremely bloody, and thousands of people had been killed and wounded. Iraq renamed the city Khuninshahr—the City of Blood.

The Iraqis also attacked Abadan, site of a major oil installation in Iran, but they could not capture that city.

In mid-November 1980, two months after it had begun, the war hit a stalemate. Both countries increased their armies, but the onset of winter made fighting impossible. Winter rains and spring flooding from melting snows in the Zagros Mountains made the roads impassable and turned the terrain to mud, making travel impossible in much of Khuzestan.

In January 1981, the Iranians attacked the Susangerd region. The Iranians were defeated, and both nations lost many men and suffered extensive damage to artillery and equipment. In May 1981, the Iranians did manage to take Susangerd, but in September of the same year, they were forced to lift the siege of Abadan, and so they were not able to turn the tide of the war.

In addition to the tribulations of war, the Iranians experienced political turmoil in 1981. President Bani-Sadr was ousted and flown from Iran to Paris. Following assassinations and bombings by anti-revolutionary forces, elections were held. Hojatolislam Mohammed Ali Khameini was elected president of Iran.

Early in 1982, the war took on a different character. In March, Iran launched a major offensive against Dezful, a town in Khuzestan. The code name of this offensive was "Undeniable Victory." Iran used many tactics, including "human wave attacks" by the Pasdaran, the Revolutionary Guards. (A human wave attack is an attack designed to overwhelm the enemy by the use of sheer numbers of soldiers sent into battle.) The Pasdaran, many of whom are

The ruins of the city of Khorramshahr
after an Iraqi air raid, 1980

Iraqi missile attack on Abadan

children, are willing to go on suicide missions. Their eagerness is akin to that of the Japanese kamikaze pilots of World War II.

Saudi Arabia, Jordan, and other Gulf states wanted the Iraqis to win the war. They even provided Iraq with some $20 billion in loans to aid the war effort. In the spirit of Pan-Arabism—unity among Arabs of all nations—King Hussein of Jordan sent "symbolic" volunteers to assist Iraq. In response to this outside support of Iraq, the Ayatollah Khomeini warned the Persian Gulf countries: "Do not do anything which will oblige us, under the tenets of the Koran, to treat you according to divine law." The other Gulf nations feared Iran would attack oil terminals, refineries, and pipelines throughout the region.

In May 1982, Iranian forces recaptured the city of Khorramshahr and reinstated its old name. Thousands of Iranians celebrated in the streets of Teheran, and, as they had at other times during the war, claimed that their victory was a sign of God's support, and that Hussein would soon be toppled. But by 1983, the war had reached a stalemate once again.

In the spring of 1984, numerous attacks by Iran and Iraq on international ships in the Persian Gulf caused alarm. Also, several countries, including Saudi Arabia, were concerned that Iran's Shi'ite revolution would spread throughout the Gulf where there are many members of that Islamic sect. Several analysts predicted worldwide involvement if the Iranians blocked the Strait of Hormuz, as they had threatened to do.

Iraq blockaded the island of Kharg, Iran's main oil terminal, to prevent Iran from selling oil. The Iraqis hoped that Iran would be unable to buy arms and equipment for the war if it had no revenue from oil sales.

Iran retaliated by bombing tankers that had stopped in Kuwait, Saudi Arabia, and other Arab nations in the Gulf. This stage of the conflict was known as the shipping

Young Iranian soldiers. Tens of thousands of teenage Iranians have volunteered to serve at the front. Notice the picture of Khomeini on the rifle above.

war, or the tanker war. By the end of 1984, sixty ships had been attacked in the Persian Gulf by both nations.

During 1984, Iraq was reported to have used mustard gas, as well as a nerve gas invented by the Germans in 1936. Many nations criticized Iraq for its use of chemical warfare.

Still, Iraq offered to negotiate an end to the war. But Iran declined and demanded $150 billion in reparations and the expulsion of President Hussein as conditions to end the conflict.

In the spring of 1985, the fighting was concentrated around Basra and other civilian areas. Then Khomeini called for a continuation of the war and swore that Iran would deal Iraq a "final blow."

Both nations claimed victory in their struggle over control of a highway that links the Iraqi capital of Baghdad with Basra. However, it is hard to know who really won this conflict—or any other, in fact—because Iraq and Iran both claim victory in nearly every confrontation. Iran had attempted to break the military deadlock, but it was apparently overwhelmed by Iraqi troops.

In a battle that raged for a week in the Huwaizah marshes, it was estimated that of 30,000 to 50,000 Iranian soldiers engaged in the fighting, most were killed, captured, or wounded. Iran did not acknowledge its loss, however, and instead claimed a victory. Although Iraq won this round of fighting, the victory is unlikely to alter the course of the war decisively.

In the phase of the conflict known as "the war of the cities," Iran attacked Baghdad. The Iranians claim that they used Soviet-made surface-to-surface missiles known as Scud B's to attack Baghdad. (Those weapons have a 185-mile [296 km] range, and Baghdad is only about 75 miles [120 km] from the Iranian border.)

Within two weeks eight explosions had damaged highways, hotels, and banks in Baghdad, although few citizens were killed. The Iraqi government maintained the first two

Oil tanker on fire

Above: *a wall painting in Iran memorializes
a battle.* Left: *Iraqi soldiers in foxholes during
an Iranian air attack.*

Iranian soldiers clearing a mine field

blasts were the work of saboteurs, but the others were definitely caused by missiles launched by Iran.

At this same time, the Iraqis bombed Teheran and other Iranian cities in an attempt to force Iran to surrender and end the war. Then the Iraqis issued an ultimatum: total peace or total war.

The two nations blamed each other for breaking a 1984 agreement arranged by the U.N. In that agreement, both nations had promised not to raid civilian areas.

Over the years, several nations and groups including the United Nations, the Islamic Conference Organization, Turkey, Pakistan, Algeria, and India have attempted to bring an end to the war through negotiations. Both the United States and the Soviet Union have urged a settlement, but the war has continued.

A pattern of fighting has emerged over the years. A series of spring offensives will take place, followed by counteroffensives that lead to a stalemate. Each country has approximately 500,000 troops. In Iran, about half of the soldiers are members of the Revolutionary Guard, the Pasdaran. Many experts say that Iraq has a better army, yet Iran's determination to continue the war seems undiminished.

Recently after the Iraqis attacked Dezful, Iranian survivors shouted "War until victory." Members of the youthful Pasdaran go to their death as willing martyrs. They are given plastic keys to ensure their entrance into heaven in accordance with the tenets of Shi'a Islam. The Iranians often send in the Pasdaran to clear mine fields in place of sweeping devices.

But if there is fanaticism and a refusal to give up in Iran, there is also an unwillingness in Iraq to end the conflict.

The war seems far from a final solution. Experts forecast a lasting stalemate between the two nations with sporadic outbursts of fighting.

CHAPTER
FIVE
THE ECONOMICS
OF WAR

By 1981 the Iran-Iraq conflict had already proved to be one of the costliest border wars in history. Some analysts speculated that at that point the damage had already reached a figure in the tens of billions of dollars.

Cities and towns were destroyed, and people were killed, captured, and maimed. Industry and oil facilities in both countries were ruined. Oil revenues were lost. Iraq's foreign exchange reserves were exhausted.

ON THE EVE
OF DESTRUCTION

Iran's prewar economy was weak as a result of the 1979 revolution. Three factors contributed to the problem. First, the government practiced a generally unwise economic policy. Second, the government poorly handled oil policies. Third, the United States froze all Iranian foreign reserves as retribution for the hostage crisis.

The Iranian economy, which had declined in the last few months of the Shah's regime, continued to falter after the revolutionaries seized control. The ayatollah's regime declared that Iran was about to enter a period of expansion and growth. Instead, industry ran at only about 50 percent capacity. Some experts estimate that unemployment in Iran was as high as 30 to 50 percent before the war began.

Under Khomeini, Iran's oil production also declined. Before the ayatollah's takeover, Iran was producing an average of 6 million barrels of oil a day. In 1978, the average dropped to 5.2. In 1979, that average dropped to 3.1 million barrels. At first, the decline in production was not considered significant. It did not affect revenues, because oil prices had increased. In fact, the price of oil had risen *because* of the revolution. Buyers feared oil shortages, and they panicked. The race was on to buy more oil, and the greater demand resulted in higher prices.

However, by early 1980, Iranian oil sales declined for several reasons. First, a worldwide recession caused a decrease in the demand for oil. Second, there was a greater trend toward the use of other fuels, such as coal, nuclear, and solar power, and people began to conserve oil. Third, several countries lowered the price of their oil so that the more expensive Iranian oil was less desirable. Finally, there was unrest among the oil workers in Iran, and some Iranian pipelines and oil fields were sabotaged. The result of all these circumstances was a loss in oil sales for Iran.

The Iranian economy was also damaged when the United States tried to exert pressure to end the hostage crisis. Before the American embassy was seized in Teheran, Iranian foreign exchange reserves totaled approximately $15 billion. Of that total, $11 billion was in U.S.-controlled banks. Since Iran had no access to these funds, many countries refused to trade with Iran. In addition, the trade embargo imposed by the United States further weakened Iran's position. Raw materials and consumer products, already in short supply in Iran, became scarcer.

In contrast to the bad situation in Iran, Iraq was experiencing growth and prosperity in 1980. In fact, Iraq took advantage of Iran's oil production problems to become the second largest producer and exporter of oil in OPEC (Organization of Petroleum Exporting Countries). Iraqi

*The American Embassy in Teheran under
occupation by militant Iranians, 1979.
The seizure of the embassy and the
hostage crisis that followed resulted in the
"freezing" of Iranian assets in U.S. banks.
This action by the United States placed
a tremendous economic strain on Iran.*

oil production increased from 2.6 to 3.5 million barrels a day. Revenues doubled between 1978 and 1979. Wages rose, and at the same time more consumer goods, especially imports, became available. Under President Hussein's strong economic policies, Iraqis were able to surround themselves with Western conveniences and luxuries, such as refrigerators and television sets. Iraqi foreign exchange reserves were higher than they had ever been before. Some estimate that Iraq had nearly $30 billion dollars in foreign accounts.

THE ECONOMIC EFFECTS
OF THE WAR

Much of the economic impact of the war has been felt in the oil industry. Not only have major oil installations suffered damage, but Iran and Iraq may have lost hundreds of billions of dollars in revenues.

Major oil production sites were the targets of attack in both countries. Abadan, Iran's largest oil refinery, was shut down early in the war. Before that time, it had produced about 630,000 barrels a day.

Iraq attempted to devastate Iran's oil economy further by blockading Kharg Island. Tankers and ships within 50 miles (80 km) of the oil terminal were struck. If foreign tankers were unable to load Iranian oil, perhaps Iran would be deprived of money to buy weapons and supplies from other countries. This was Iraq's hope and fervent wish. Baghdad declared it would "tighten the blockade of Kharg Island until Teheran's rulers choke to death because they can no longer breathe through their only lung, Kharg." But the main effect of Iraq's blockade of Kharg Island was the tripling of insurance rates on oil shipped through the Persian Gulf.

Iraq suffered losses at Basra, an important oil-producing region, as well as at the terminals of Mina al-Baqr, which had a prewar capacity of about 2.5 million barrels. By 1984, Iraq's oil industry was more heavily battered than

Iran's. Iraq was unable to ship oil through the Persian Gulf, and instead had to send it through a pipeline that extended through Turkey to the Mediterranean Sea. Figures for oil production vary considerably, but four years after the start of the war, Iraq was thought to be producing about 1 million barrels a day while Iran turned out approximately 1.6 million barrels a day. These figures represent substantial drop-offs in production.

Both Iran and Iraq have suffered losses in other industries as well. Chemical, steel, and iron plants located in the war zone were heavily shelled. There have been shortages in electricity, fuel, and spare parts. The available pool of workers has diminished as thousands of men marched off to the front lines to fight.

For some time Iraq was able to carry on a five-year plan conceived during its period of economic expansion. The $135 billion spending measure called for the construction of subways, railroads, highways, and bridges. But the huge expense of the war brought Iraq's government project to a halt.

By 1983, Iraq was calling for donations of gold from its people. Citizens waited outside government offices carrying gold jewelry and coins, which were weighed and counted. As a result, the government collected an estimated 30 tons of gold and millions of dinars to help cover the cost of the war. Soldiers often asked Iraqis to show their receipts as proof that they had donated to the cause. Foreigners who worked in Iraq were expected to contribute as well. The prevailing philosophy was that if one earned a salary in Iraq, then one must return the favor by contributing to the cause.

In addition to the severe damage Iraq's industries have experienced, its once healthy foreign exchange reserves were cut in half to about $16 billion. Iraq sought bank loans from other countries and credit on trades.

By 1984 some members of the Gulf Cooperation Council, primarily Saudi Arabia and Kuwait, had given

Iranian oil wells burning

Iraqi prisoners of war

A refugee camp

An Iranian woman mourning her son

Iraq interest-free loans amounting to approximately $35 billion. The loans were to help pay the cost of the war. One reason these countries lent money to Iraq was that they believed an Iraqi victory was in the interest of Pan-Arabism. A second, but no less important reason for their support of Iraq was the fear that an Iranian victory would result in the exportation of Shi'ite revolution throughout the Gulf. If this happened the entire region—including Saudi Arabia and Kuwait—could be embroiled in anarchy and unrest.

VICTIMS OF THE WAR

By 1984 it was reported that there were one million refugees in the Iranian province of Khuzestan. Some 300,000 Iranian soldiers and 250,000 Iraqi troops had been killed, captured, or wounded. Among the injured were Iranian soldiers who sustained burns, blisters, and lung damage from Iraqi chemical weapons.

Houses, bridges, hotels, and roads had been destroyed, and even more were reduced to rubble in the "war of the cities." When the smoke cleared, and the confusion of sirens and ambulances stopped, deaths and injuries were catalogued.

Experts believe there will be many more victims in the future as the endless fighting continues to take its toll. Considering the ravaged economies of both countries, future generations of Iraqis and Iranians are likely to suffer greatly, too.

CHAPTER
SIX
REGIONAL COMPLICATIONS

When the Shah of Iran fell from power, leaders of other Gulf states began to worry about the stability of their own regimes. The ouster of the Shah, who had been so powerful and wealthy, was a grim reminder of the weakness of all monarchies.

These leaders, as we said before, were also afraid that Iran's Shi'ite revolution would spread to their countries. Based on the populations in the region, it seemed a very real possibility. In Qatar, 30 percent of the population are Shi'as; in Kuwait, 30 to 40 percent belong to the radical Islamic sect. More than 50 percent of the population of Bahrain is Shi'a. In Saudi Arabia some 200,000 Shi'as live in the eastern oil-producing region.

From Iran's point of view, the Sunni Muslims who control Gulf politics do not subscribe to an authentic form of Islam. Moreover, Iranians do not approve of Arab links to the West, and assert the "godless" regimes ought to be overturned. In October 1980, one month after the conflict between Iran and Iraq began, Iran's former Islamic Republican party leader Ali Khameini said: "We are determined to send Saddam [Hussein] to hell. His collaborators' turn will come later. I am referring to the Shaykhs in the Gulf region, and some rulers in the Arab region. The

*The Shah of Iran and Empress Farah left Iran
in January 1979. A soldier bends to kiss the
feet of the departing monarch. The Shah flew
to Mexico and then to the United States where
he was treated for cancer. His arrival in the
U.S. helped bring about the hostage crisis.
The Shah died in 1980 in Egypt.*

Shaykhs have betrayed Islam and the Koran." Iran had had no qualms about taking on the United States, either. To the countries in the Gulf region, threats from Teheran coupled with Iranian anger and hatred were serious matters.

THE GULF
COOPERATION COUNCIL

For several years, Arab nations had sought to form an alliance that would benefit the people of all the Gulf states. The proposed league would assist in bringing order to the nations' economic, industrial, educational, immigration, and banking systems. It would also regulate travel and, most important, develop strategies for defense and security.

The Iran-Iraq War confirmed the need for such a group and, in February 1981, the Gulf Cooperation Council (GCC) was formed. The members were Saudi Arabia, Kuwait, Oman, Qatar, Bahrain, and the United Arab Emirates. Iran and Iraq were not asked to join because they were at war. In any case, there would have been some debate about Iraq's membership because President Hussein clearly wanted to hold the power in the Gulf region. Also, the other Arab nations speculated that Iraq might attempt to control the council. As time went on, Iraq's links to the Gulf states grew closer, and Iran was seen as the far greater threat. Fears that Iran was likely to destabilize the entire region and bring economic ruin down on all led the GCC to support Iraq. To date, members of the GCC, including Saudi Arabia, Kuwait, the United Arab Emirates, and Qatar have lent some $35 billion to Iraq to help in the war effort against Iran.

Although the GCC is not a defense pact, regional security is a most important issue. Some of the Gulf nations greatly need to be protected from the spread of the war. In fact, all are concerned that the war may spill over into their territory. Reproaches and warnings have been aired publicly. In 1984, Iranian President Khameini declared:

"We do not ask the Gulf States to support us, and we do not expect any help except from God and our people. But we ask them to take a neutral position. If they take the opposite position, it is natural they must face the consequences. This is inevitable."

The GCC adopted a united Arab stand against Iran. In order to provide some measure of defense against the possibility of attack, it assembled about 100 patrol craft. At the same time, members of the council desire to remain uninvolved. But the war is just twenty minutes from their borders. Security, therefore, is a vital issue in the Gulf states.

IRAQ'S ALLIES

BAHRAIN AND OMAN

Bahrain is the only island state in the Gulf region and is the poorest. Its government is dominated by Sunni Arabs, yet almost three-fourths of its population consists of Shi'ite Muslims. In December 1981, seventy Bahraini nationalists and twelve Shi'ite Saudis and their cohorts attempted a coup. It was thought that Iran was involved in the attempted takeover. This event aggravated worries about the export of Iran's revolution to the other Gulf nations.

Oman is a nation located on the Arabian Peninsula. It was anxious about the Iranian revolution because it had received help from the Shah in putting down an internal revolt. Because Oman is strategically located on the Strait of Hormuz, its people feared that Iran would attack them in retribution after Oman supported the Shah. This fear caused Oman to seek assistance from the United States. It is now America's strongest ally in the Gulf region.

JORDAN

Jordan is a small kingdom bordered by Syria and Iraq. (Don't confuse its King Hussein with President Hussein of Iraq.) King Hussein of Jordan was alarmed about the overthrow of the Shah and the collapse of Iran's monarchy.

He understood that unrest can hurt and ultimately dethrone a monarch. Some analysts attribute Jordan's support of Iraq to the friendship between the two rulers. Another tie exists, however, in that Iraq and Jordan, being next-door neighbors, share the Jordanian port of Aqaba, part of which was leased to Iraq for its sole use. The profits from Aqaba were used to develop the port and to construct roads between Aqaba and Iraq, so the ties between the two nations are economic as well as geographical and political.

KUWAIT

Kuwait is a small country that lies south of Iraq and west of Iran. It also shares a border with Saudi Arabia to the south. Kuwait is only ten minutes flying time from an Iranian air base. Hence, it is the most vulnerable of the Gulf states. Kuwait has had difficulties in the past with both of its larger, more powerful neighbors. Iraq has made claims on Kuwaiti territory, although much of the tension involving that situation has dissipated. And Iran was suspected in the bombing of the French and American embassies in Kuwait in 1983. In addition, Kuwait has suffered from Iranian and Iraqi attacks on its oil facilities as well as on its tankers.

In 1984 during the shipping war, tankers had to maneuver through the war zone to reach Kuwait. As a result of the attacks, insurance rates rose from .25 percent of the value of the freight to 1 percent. The increase added about 30 cents a barrel to the cost of Kuwaiti oil. Although it may not seem to be a large increase, Kuwaiti oil sales can be affected by even a slight change, because more than half of its exports are sold on the spot oil market. This means oil is sold at a certain price with a short-term delivery date.

*Sultan Qabus bin Said of Oman
and President Reagan*

Because the spot market fluctuates rapidly and wildly, the potential for loss to the seller is great.

EGYPT

In March 1979 Egypt made peace with Israel after years of war. Almost unanimously, the Arab states, including Iraq, angrily ended diplomatic relations with Egypt. They also dismissed Egypt from the Arab League and cut off all aid to that nation.

Former Egyptian President Anwar Sadat was critical of the Iran-Iraq war, yet he supplied arms to Iraq by way of Jordan. He also declared that Egypt would help any Arab country that desired military backing. Clearly, Sadat wanted to have friendly relations with the Arab nations, and analysts believe most Arabs, in turn, thought a strong Egypt would be good for regional stability.

In the spring of 1985, President Hosni Mubarak of Egypt went to Baghdad with King Hussein of Jordan to demonstrate Egypt's interest in promoting Pan-Arabism. Many experts thought his visit would help repair the tattered friendship between Iraq and Egypt.

SAUDI ARABIA

Saudi Arabia is the largest exporter of oil in the world and has foreign reserves of $100 billion. It is the biggest of the nations in the Gulf Cooperation Council. Saudi Arabia is thought of as a rich and powerful nation. Media portraits of wealthy sheikhs buying expensive items in exclusive shops and living in palatial homes the world over give people that impression. Yet some analysts note that Saudi Arabia has neither great economic strength nor great power.

The per capita income of Saudi Arabia is actually lower than that of Finland. Oil, which provides the biggest chunk of Saudi revenues—10 million barrels flow daily from Saudi facilities—has made it a likely site for military attacks. Moreover, during the past few years, the Saudis have depended heavily on a small number of countries for imports and exports. It also has to import its high-tech equipment. All of this means that Saudi Arabia is not a very self-sufficient nation.

Some experts also believe that Saudi Arabia is not a powerful nation. Its relatively small population of six million translates into too little manpower. Its military capabilities are slight as well. The Saudis have expressed genuine fears about the Iran-Iraq war. In 1981, at the Saudis' request, the United States sent them four AWACS (Airborne Warning and Control Systems) planes. At that time, Iraq was annoyed by Saudi-U.S. cooperation.

By 1984 Saudi Arabia and Iraq had become friendlier, and Iran was seen as the real threat to the Gulf region when it attacked Saudi and Kuwaiti tankers.

The Saudis called for a united Arab front against non-Arab Iran, and issued the following warning: "Any aggression against a GCC member is aggression against them all." The Saudis hoped to ensure the safety and stability of the Gulf region without being drawn into the Iran-Iraq conflict. The Saudis also requested U.S. support, and President Reagan responded by sending 400 Stinger anti-aircraft missiles to Saudi Arabia. The Saudis wanted the weapons, but were suspicious of additional U.S. intervention.

IRAN'S SUPPORTERS

SYRIA

Because it borders Iraq, Syria is close to the conflict and has been Iran's principal ally. Syria's leaders are Alawite Muslim, a sort of offshoot of Shi'ism, and they sympathize with the revolutionary government. In addition, the Alawites probably identify with the Shi'as because both groups are minority Muslims among the Sunni Arabs.

It is possible that Syria supports Iran because Syria fears isolation in the Arab world if Iraq wins the war. Syria is hostile toward Iraq as a result of rivalry between the two segments of the Ba'ath party in both nations.

LIBYA

A large desert nation on the Mediterranean coast of Africa, Libya disapproves of Iraq's nonmilitant position regarding Israel's raids into Lebanon. The Libyans also were angry when Iraq accepted Egypt's renewed peace with Israel. Some experts think Libya strongly approves of Iran's revolution and its radical ideologies.

SOUTH YEMEN

This nation on the Arabian Peninsula is still an enemy of Iraq because the Iraqis supported North Yemen when the two Yemens fell out. Iraq apparently sided with North Yemen because it had many adherents of the Iraqi Ba'ath party. Whatever the reason, South Yemen is now a supporter of Iran.

Iraq has been able to garner more support in the Gulf than Iran. President Hussein, to be sure, is a dictator, but he does not engender the same fear and resentment as the vengeful, radical Ayatollah Khomeini. Hussein is also an Arab, which has made it easier for the Gulf states to close ranks against Khomeini, who has threatened and compromised their governments, their stability, their security, and their way of life.

About 60 percent of the world's oil comes from the Gulf region. If the other nations were to be drawn into the Iran-Iraq war, the damage to the oil market could be very great.

Although fears about serious oil shortages have subsided, the risk is always present. Indeed, these worries have fallen and risen along with Iranian defeats and gains in the war.

Because Iran is so warlike and threatens any and all opponents, there is always a possibility of regional involvement.

Drastic cutbacks in oil availability translate into world-wide economic hardship. Prices climb as demands rise, and they can skyrocket overnight. Inflation, industrial slumps with accompanying unemployment—all happen quickly. Depression sets in and worsens the situation. These economic nightmares are the main reason the Gulf is vital to America and Europe. The Gulf's pipelines have become the lifelines to the West's business, industry, and economy.

If the other Gulf nations join in the Iran-Iraq war, there is a chance that one or more of the superpowers will step in, too. And intervention from the Soviet Union or the United States is something the Saudis and the other Gulf nations clearly want to avoid.

CHAPTER
SEVEN
THE SUPERPOWERS

When the war broke out between Iraq and Iran, there was a general fear in the West that the conflict would result in reduced oil output from the region. Former President Jimmy Carter proclaimed the United States would remain neutral, but he also said that the United States was prepared to use military force if necessary to protect Gulf oil supplies from outside threats. The Carter administration was disturbed because the Soviet Union had diplomatic relations with both Iran and Iraq and had been the main supplier of military equipment to Iraq.

At the same time, the hostage crisis of 1979 further complicated the issue. Carter offered to send to Iran some $240 million worth of spare parts the Iranians had bought from the United States but had not yet received. In exchange for the spare parts, Carter asked for a guarantee of the safe release of the fifty-four American hostages held at the embassy in Teheran.

When Ronald Reagan became President, he continued Carter's policies. The United States remained neutral but began to build up a Rapid Deployment Force—a quick-response military unit. Reagan refused to ship to Iran the spare parts that Carter had promised. Reagan also refused to sell equipment the Iranians wanted in order to refurbish

American F-14 planes they had purchased during the reign of the Shah.

As Iraq became less radical and more moderate, the United States began to show more sympathy toward that nation. Iraq moved closer to Jordan and Saudi Arabia, and at the same time moved away from the Soviet Union. Its name was removed from the U.S. list of countries known to assist terrorists. As a result, the United States again allowed its exports to go to Iraq.

In 1984, when the war between Iran and Iraq was nearly four years old, frequent attacks on tankers in the Persian Gulf raised concerns once again that the war would spread. U.S. State Department spokesman John Hughes declared: "The United States reiterates our firm belief that attacks on international shipping in the Persian Gulf represent a dangerous escalation of the Iran-Iraq war, and a growing threat to freedom of navigation in the Persian Gulf." The United States maintained its neutrality, but declared that the Persian Gulf is an "area of vital interest to us; we are prepared to defend our vital interests."

The United States also offered air cover to thwart the attacks on the oil tankers, but told the Gulf nations it would need airfields, radar, and warehouses in order to provide effective protection. In addition, the United States offered to help the Gulf states plan for military emergencies. Also, if the Gulf States requested it, the United States said it would use Western ships to escort oil tankers. The U.S. took these actions to prevent the closing of the Gulf and to ensure the continuation of oil shipments.

The United States sent Saudi Arabia KC-10 aerial tankers, 400 Stingers (anti-aircraft missiles with a three-mile range), and 200 missile launchers. The Saudis had requested the weapons because they were alarmed about the potential of the Gulf war.

But, in general, the Gulf States were wary of the U.S. offers for several reasons. First, the Persian Gulf nations feared that American assistance might make them targets of

The USS Luce *in Bahrain's harbor.*
The United States has helped strengthen defense systems
around the Persian Gulf and aims to safeguard the
shipment of oil through the Strait of Hormuz.

Iranian or Syrian attacks. Second, some of the Gulf states believed U.S. intervention might lead to Soviet involvement, with the result that the Gulf countries would be caught in a net of rivalry between the two superpowers. And third, the Arab nations are fiercely determined to maintain their independence.

Of all the Gulf nations, Kuwait was the most outspoken in turning down American offers of assistance. Anti-American outcries were frequent, and Kuwait said the United States had instigated Iranian threats in an attempt to force frightened Gulf countries to ask for U.S. help. Experts felt that Kuwait, in its fear of both Iraq and Iran, made an error in accusing the United States.

There is no doubt that the Persian Gulf states are suspicious of U.S. aid and assistance. In a similar vein, some analysts believe the United States would be more likely to end the war by reducing its military involvement than by increasing its military presence. They maintain that aerial fueling for Saudi planes, stationing aircraft carriers, such as the *Kitty Hawk*, in the Arabian Sea, flying U.S. radar planes, and allowing the export of weapons to the warring countries constitutes military pressure.

Experts urge the United States to seek alternative methods of curtailing and containing the Iran-Iraq war. Suggestions included (1) purchasing less oil from the combatants while at the same time buying more oil from other suppliers; (2) assisting with the construction of a pipeline that would do away with much of the current dependency on shipping in the Gulf; and (3) discouraging military and financial assistance to both Iran and Iraq from other countries. Without financial backing, the experts feel Iran and Iraq would be forced to end the war. Many officials recommend that the United States use imaginative diplomatic solutions as a means to bring the war to an end.

The United States had no direct influence in either Iran or Iraq until it established diplomatic relations with Baghdad in 1984. In 1985, Washington attempted to convince

Iran of the near impossibility of a military victory. The United States continues to insist that it does not provide arms to either side. But it has recently tried to prevent Iran from getting more weapons because Iran has refused to negotiate any settlement to the war. Officials hope that if its supplies are cut off, Iran will stop fighting. At the same time, the United States has criticized Iraq for using poison gas and chemical weapons. Iraq agreed to desist from using chemical warfare when it agreed to the terms of the Geneva Protocol in 1931, but it scorns those agreements in the conflict with Iran.

SOVIET POLICY

Unlike the United States, the Soviet Union has its own oil wells and therefore has not been concerned about the availability of oil as a result of the Gulf War. At the same time, the Soviet Union has had a treaty of friendship and accord with Iraq since 1972. Some experts believe that the Soviets approved of the severe anti-American rhetoric of the revolutionaries in Iran. Like the United States, the Soviet Union remains neutral in the Iran-Iraq war, but when the first AWACS were sent to Saudi Arabia during the Carter era, the Soviets criticized the U.S. action. While they censured the American action, however, a Soviet fleet of twelve combat vessels and seventeen support ships was stationed in the region.

At the start of the war, the Soviets were aloof toward Iraq and warm toward Iran. Several incidents led to the deterioration of Soviet-Iraq relations from the late 1970s on.

First, as Iraq became less radical, the Ba'ath party government decided to reduce the number of soldiers who would receive military training in the Soviet Union. Apparently, Iraq was concerned about the soldiers' Marxist indoctrination. Second, in 1978, the Iraqi government executed twenty-one communists for allegedly attempting to subvert the Iraqi army. The Soviet Union, Bulgaria, and

A chemical bomb

*Iran's Revolutionary Guards and volunteer tank hunters
use motorcycles to locate and destroy Iraqi tanks.*

East Germany tried to stop the executions, but they failed. A third episode that may have antagonized the Soviets occurred in 1981 when the Ba'ath Party refused to send delegates to a Communist party congress.

As its relations with Iraq became distinctly icy, Moscow thawed toward Iran. In October 1980, one month after the war began, Soviet leader Leonid Brezhnev met with Syrian President Hafez al-Assad in Moscow. They did not discuss the Gulf conflict; rather, the focus of the talks centered on praise for Iran and its revolution. Many experts believe that the Soviet Union hoped to take advantage of American-Iranian antagonism over the hostage crisis but was unable to do so. The Soviets offered to send arms, but Iran refused them.

In time, Moscow became more and more displeased about Iran's anti-Soviet remarks. Iran had referred to the USSR as "one of the two threats—that from the North" (the threat from the south being, of course, the United States).

Soviet-Iranian relations worsened in February 1983, when seventy members of Iran's communistic Tudeh party were arrested as Russian spies. In April of that year, Iran's Islamic regime dissolved the Tudeh party and ordered eight Soviet diplomats to leave the country.

The Soviets were soon able to reforge their old links with Iraq, and about two-thirds of Iraqi military equipment is now produced in the Soviet Union. In 1984, both Iran and Iraq were getting Soviet aid, and both had Soviet military advisers. Moscow was no longer courting Iran, however, and had, in fact, urged the Iranians to negotiate a settlement to the war. Interestingly enough, Iran's deputy prime minister, Tariq Aziz, is reported to have commented, "Be assured Iran will eventually be pro-American. Americans are at least Christians and less dirty for the mullahs than the atheist Soviets." Perhaps Moscow is less interested in Iran because Iran has spurned the USSR.

GULF RELATIONS
AND STRATEGIES

Until 1979, Iran was considered the keystone of the Gulf—a diplomatic prize coveted by both the United States and the Soviet Union. After the Iranian revolution, however, attention shifted to Saudi Arabia, also valued because of its strategic geographical position and abundant natural resources. But diplomatic loyalties shift often. In 1985, Oman became a new center of American attention in the Persian Gulf.

One reason for this new friendship centers on past Saudi reluctance to provide the United States with air bases. In addition, twenty American, British, and Arab advisers were able to bring influence to bear on Sultan Qabus bin Said, the sultan of Oman.

Oman is a sultanate on the Arabian Peninsula with a population of 1 to 1.5 million. After Saudi Arabia, Oman is the second largest in area of the states along the Persian Gulf and the adjoining Gulf of Oman. Oman has a small enclave on the Strait of Hormuz. It is considered critical to the West. The country staunchly maintains its Arab character: Omanis wear robes, and senior officials wear turbans and *khanjars*—silver daggers. Sultan Qabus bin Said has dictated that new buildings in the capital of Muscat must be constructed to conform to traditional Arab architecture.

In 1980, the United States signed an agreement with Oman to permit American access to military bases located there. The United States in turn promised to provide funds to update four Omani military bases. Approximately $250 million has already been spent to upgrade the Omani bases, and modernization is expected to be finished by the fall of 1986.

In the past, Oman has allowed American planes to use its bases and has engaged in joint military operations with the United States. Oman welcomes U.S. relations because it fears Soviet involvement in the Gulf.

Diplomatic relationships change over time. Soviet relations with Iran and Iraq, for example, have swung back and forth, alternately improving and worsening. The United States, too, has had to maneuver carefully. When the Shah was in power, there was friendship between Iran and the United States. But the radical activities of Khomeini's regime after the revolution damaged U.S. relations with Iran. Conversely, the American relationship with Iraq has improved as the Ba'ath party has moved closer to Western ideologies.

Both the United States and the Soviet Union have been careful to remain neutral in the Iran-Iraq War. Both combatants use Russian *and* American-made equipment. (Iran got its U.S.-manufactured supplies when the Shah was in power.) But the Soviets do not want the war to spread. Both Moscow and Washington seek an end to the fighting.

CHAPTER
EIGHT
NEGOTIATIONS

There is no lack of willing intermediaries in the conflicts over the Shatt-al-Arab River. Great Britain and Russia have been trying to settle the bloody warfare since the nineteenth century. When the old dispute flared up again in 1980, the dangers of the situation were immediately apparent. Several mediators quickly offered their assistance on the grounds that the stability of the Gulf is important to the entire world.

But a whole series of complicated issues have prevented successful negotiations. Difficulties have been multiplied and confounded by the intractability of both Iraq and Iran.

One problem is that both countries claim to be innocent victims. One week after the war began, the U.N. Security Council passed a resolution calling for a cease-fire. Iraq agreed, but Iran spurned the resolution. Iran also demanded that the United Nations censure Iraq for starting the war. Iraq, of course, claims that Iran started it. Similarly, each insists that the other was first to break the promise not to raid civilian areas.

A second problem is the two nations' mutual mistrust and suspicion. They continually hurl accusations back and forth, blaming each other for all kinds of incidents. Iraq, for example, claims Iran was responsible for the demonstrations that occurred in Shi'ite shrine cities in 1979. Iran denies the charge and counterclaims that Iraq was responsible for a series of pipeline explosions.

This strong mutual mistrust and suspicion are certain to make negotiations difficult, if not impossible. Iran has been especially uncooperative, constantly blaming Iraq for everything and insisting on its own innocence. Iran has rejected all settlement offers that did not name Iraq as the true culprit in starting the war. If both sides continue to claim innocence and refuse to take the blame, it will be difficult to reach compromises that could settle the conflict.

The Islamic Conference Organization tried to intervene early on, as did the United Nations. Problems arose because Iran accused the U.N. of being pro-Iraqi and pro-American and therefore unqualified to consider Iranian complaints, issues, or interests.

Negotiation efforts were stalled, in part, because neither Iran nor Iraq had sustained enough losses to feel concessions were worthwhile. Giving up claims to the Shatt seemed worse than the possibility of losing equipment, oil facilities, and human lives. The loss of human life was considered especially unimportant in Iran, whose population is three times that of Iraq. Thus, Iran has a large and zealous supply of manpower from which to draw its armies.

By the end of 1982, Iraq seemed the more willing of the two to negotiate. But Iran demanded Iraqi withdrawal, war reparations, and a reaffirmation of the 1975 Algiers Treaty. It also demanded punishment of Iraq as a condition for ending the war. Shortly afterward, in January 1983, President Saddam Hussein of Iraq said he would be willing to travel to Iran on a peace mission. He also publicly declared that Iraq would submit to arbitration of the dispute by a disinterested third party and would accept its decision as binding. Iran rejected Hussein's proposal and insisted there would be no settlement until he was removed from office. Khomeini, of course, is well known for his refusal to compromise, and it is possible that Hussein was bluffing because

The Ayatollah Khomeini greeting
relatives of Iran's war dead

he knew Khomeini would reject his offer. If not, Hussein was taking a big risk, for a mediator might have decided to place the Shatt under the jurisdiction of both countries.

In general, the positions of Iran and Iraq have remained basically the same since 1983, although Iraq has been more willing to compromise. Iran has made its major condition the destruction of President Hussein and the Ba'ath party.

In 1985, Iranian parliamentary leader Ali Akbar Hashemi Rafsanjani said Iran would not agree to a cease-fire but would abide by agreements to stop attacking oil tankers and civilian areas. Iran wanted Iraq to remove air space over Teheran from the war zone and to stop threatening airliners using the Iranian airport.

In another recent development, U.N. Secretary General Javier Pérez de Cuéllar has emerged as a figure whom both Iran and Iraq seem to trust. Pérez de Cuéllar insists that Iran consider a complete settlement of the war, not merely agreements to stop bombing cities and shelling neutral ships. The secretary general hopes to persuade Iraq to stop using chemical weapons, and he wants both sides to stop mistreating prisoners of war. Iraq contends it will agree to an all-out end to the war or to nothing at all.

Pérez de Cuéllar's determined effort to bring an end to the war may possibly result in peace. But both nations have always been willing to receive negotiators. However, they may do this only so as to *appear* to be cooperating. Although both sides have agreed to mediation efforts, neither has ever been willing to make compromises.

Some officials believe the point may finally have been reached when compromise seems less painful to the combatants than ongoing war. Troops on both sides have been slaughtered by the thousands, cities are being bombarded, and the standard of living has steadily declined.

But how much will each side be willing to compromise? The issue that seems most likely to block any settlement is the Shatt-al-Arab. An earlier negotiation team foundered on this very point. At that time, Iran was adamant: "The basis for settlement of this dispute is the 1975 Algiers Accord. Consequently there is no point in negotiating the Shatt-al-Arab again." Iran wants half the river, yet it doesn't seem likely that President Hussein would agree to return to the terms of the 1975 treaty, having fought nearly five years to contest it. Moreover, he only very reluctantly signed the 1975 treaty in the first place, and he was humiliated when Iraq was forced to concede half the Shatt.

Considering the tumultuous history of the Shatt, it seems unlikely that an agreement will be reached soon that provides a lasting solution and is satisfactory to both sides. Yet if Iran and Iraq are to exist as neighbors, they must somehow find a way to share the Shatt.

CHAPTER
NINE
THE OUTLOOK
FOR
THE FUTURE

After over five years, the roots and the reason for the continuing Iran-Iraq war are still not clear. In order to assess the situation and speculate about the outlook, we have to consider many events and circumstances. How heavily did each issue weigh in the decision to go to war? Was there one main cause of the war or did all the circumstances work together to produce the conflict? All of these issues can be placed in three primary categories—political, religious, and personal.

Many analysts quickly discounted the theory that Iraq began the hostilities in order to prevent Shi'a subversion and revolution. As the war has continued, the religious disagreements have assumed less and less importance, especially since no major insurrection has materialized. Yet Iran's parliamentary leader recently noted that the "pivotal point of the revolution is the zeal of the people." And other experts feel that the religious explanation, which is difficult for Westerners to identify with, has been brushed aside too easily.

Certainly, the Shi'ites clearly stated their Pan-Islamic goals. Moreover, it is obvious that the fanaticism of the Iranians is something to be reckoned with. It is, in fact, one important reason why the war has continued so long.

*A volunteer collects money and jewelry
for the Iranian war effort.*

Iraq has superior military skill and is expected to easily defeat Iran; yet it has won no decisive military victory. For their part, the Iranians have shown a fierce will to continue the war. The Pasdaran march off on suicide missions, and citizens stampede the streets after every victory to cheer and praise God and their cause.

Is this zeal solely the result of propaganda? Certainly isolation, censorship of the press, and indoctrination reinforce Iranian feelings and beliefs, but one must take into account the sincerity of many, if not most, Shi'ite Muslims.

Khomeini, of course, has been fanatically loyal to the cause, to nationalism, and to public zeal. If Iranians take their cue from him, they have found many examples of the will to continue fighting. Khomeini has adamantly insisted on certain conditions to end the war. Even at times when it appears the Iraqis might win, Khomeini has not altered his position, or indicated that Iran will surrender or cease the fighting.

Some experts believe the war is more political than religious. The chief issue is the Shatt-al-Arab; yet others feel that the Shatt issue may not prove quite so thorny as it has in the past. Iraq has been shipping oil overland, and since Iraq claims full sovereignty over the Shatt but has been unable to use the river, it may be willing to share the waterway in the future.

Some people say that another reason for the war was a desire for political dominance in the Gulf. Both nations clearly wanted to be the most powerful in the region. Still others contend that the desire for dominance was probably not a direct cause of war. Power, they say, does not depend on winning wars. It is based on people's perceptions of the power or weakness of an opponent. Power can also be related to economics, fear, and force. Of course, some suspect Hussein may have been trying to bully Iran. He expected to win quickly, and he may have intended to use his victory as a stepping stone toward total dominance of the Gulf region. Similarly, Khomeini probably hoped for a

An Iranian shepherd watches as tanks pass by.
For the people of Iran and Iraq, the war between
their two nations has become a fact of life.

victorious Iran that would rule the Gulf unchallenged, and topple the "godless anti-republican monarchies." He may have envisioned himself as the leader of a sweeping sea of Islamic masses.

The Iran-Iraq conflict has also been described as the result of the personalities of the two leaders. Both Hussein and Khomeini are headstrong and determined. In addition, they profoundly dislike each other. Their animosity has been inflamed by the long war and the public slurs each has cast. Yet if the war were merely a personal battle being waged on a massive scale, it would end if one or the other were deposed or died. When Khomeini dies, who will take his place, a cleric or a secular leader? Perhaps a group of mullahs will take up the reins of power. Or maybe Khomeini is now grooming a successor who is acceptable to other Iranian leaders. But if so, would the new ruler or group be able to wield as much influence as Khomeini?

All of these circumstances may have contributed in some measure to the outbreak and continuation of the conflict between Iran and Iraq. The question remains, what will be the consequences of this war? There are two possible answers to this question.

One answer is optimistic and sounds like this: The Iran-Iraq War has demonstrated that a conflict in the Persian Gulf does not necessarily translate into severe oil shortages. If, after all this time, the oil market has not been devastated by the involvement of the other Arab states in the region, there is probably little likelihood of an oil trauma. In addition, as long as the region remains stable, there is very little possibility of global involvement.

The second answer is pessimistic and goes like this: Negotiations may be a long way off, and meanwhile the Iran-Iraq war should be considered potentially hazardous. One danger arises from the threat of the loss of oil; the other is the chance that the superpowers will step in. Keep in mind that even though the Soviets have their own oil supply, they would like to expand their territory into the Gulf and have already moved into nearby Afghanistan. In addition, the Soviets may desire political gains in the Gulf in order to check American interests.

What will the future be like for Iran and Iraq? Considering the economic declines that both have suffered, Iraqis and Iranians may face years of hardship. In 1984, for example, visitors to Teheran noticed that building construction had been abandoned. Iraq has spent billions to keep the war effort going, and as a result, much of its earlier progress has also gone to ruin. Iran has carried on the war with few economic resources and little help from the outside.

How soon will peace prevail and what will be the result of negotiations? As one historian has noted, wars do not end even after the last bomb has exploded and the last heap of rubble has been cleared. The repercussions of wars last for years and years. And perhaps that is the most terrible prediction of all for Iran and Iraq.

GLOSSARY

Abadan: Located in Khuzestan, this is Iran's largest oil refinery. It was shut down early in the war.

Abu Musa: A small island at the mouth of the Strait of Hormuz. It belongs to the United Arab Emirates and was seized by Iran in 1971.

Algiers Treaty: Signed by Iran and Iraq in 1975. Iraq was forced to concede half the Shatt-al-Arab. President Saddam Hussein of Iraq did away with the treaty in 1980, leading to the current conflict.

Ali Khameini, Hojatolislam: President of Iran.

al-Assad, Hafez: President of Syria.

An Najaf: A Shi'a holy city in southern Iraq.

Ba'ath Party: The secular party in Iran. It promotes Pan-Arabism, that is, the unity of all Arabs.

Baghdad: The capital of Iraq.

Bahrain: An island state in the Persian Gulf. Bahrain is a member of the Gulf Cooperation Council.

Bakhtiar, Shapur: Former prime minister of Iran. He was forced to resign during the revolution.

Bani-Sadr, Abolhassan: Former president of Iran. He was forced to flee to France during the revolution.

Basra: Iraq's most important port.

Farsi (Persian): Language of the Iranians.

Gulf Cooperation Council (GCC): An alliance consisting of Saudi Arabia, Kuwait, Oman, Qatar, Bahrain, and the United Arab Emirates.

Gulf Nations: Also called Gulf States, or Arab Gulf States; these include Iraq, Saudi Arabia, Muscat, Qatar, Kuwait, United Arab Emirates, Bahrain, and Oman. When referring to the Gulf in a general way, some authors include not only those countries, which are located on the Persian Gulf, but those which are affected because of political implications. Examples of the latter include Pakistan, Afghanistan, Turkey, and the Yemens.

Hussein, Saddam: President of Iraq.

Islam: A religion which preaches that there is one God, Allah. His prophet is Mohammed. Its followers are known as Muslims.

Karbala: A Shi'a shrine and holy city in Iraq.

Karun: Iran's most important river system.

Kharg Island: Iran's main oil terminal.

Khomeini, Ayatollah Ruhollah: Head of the Iranian government. Khomeini is a Shi'a Muslim, and has called for a return to old laws.

Khorramshahr: Port in Khuzestan.

Khuzestan: An oil-rich area in Iran. It was formerly called Arabistan.

Kurds: An ethnic group in Iran, Iraq, and Turkey. The Kurds led an insurrection in Iraq in the 1970s.

Kuwait: A small nation located at the northern end of the Persian Gulf. Kuwait is a member of the GCC.

Mojahedin: A guerrilla group that opposed Khomeini's regime in Iran.

Mubarak, Hosni: President of Egypt.

Oman: One of the Persian Gulf states, Oman has a small enclave on the Strait of Hormuz. It has recently emerged as America's strongest ally in the Gulf.

Pahlavi, Mohammed Reza: The Shah of Iran. He fled Iran in 1979 and died in Egypt in 1980.

Pan-Arabism: A concept or ideal that calls for unity among Arabs. It is secular rather than religious in orientation.

Pasdaran: The Revolutionary Guards in Iran, known for their willingness to accept suicide missions.

Qabus bin Said: The sultan and absolute ruler of Oman.

Qadissiyaa: A seventh-century battle in which the Arabs defeated the Persians (Iranians). The current war is often called Saddam's [Hussein's] Qadissiyaa.

Shah of Iran: See Pahlavi, Mohammed Reza.

Shatt-al-Arab: A river formed where the Tigris and Euphrates rivers flow together. The Shatt empties into the Persian Gulf. The river has been the site of disputes for centuries.

Shi'ism: A sect of Islam. Shi'as (or Shi'ites) and Sunnis have been at odds for centuries. This radical religious group has led the Iranian revolution.

Sunni: A sect of Islam. Sunnis control most politics in the Arab states.

Teheran: The capital of Iran.

Thalweg: The midline and deepest part of a river.

Tunbs, Greater and Lesser: Two small uninhabited islands of great strategic value. Like Abu Musa, they lie at the mouth of the Strait of Hormuz, the "oil jugular of the West."

FOR
FURTHER
READING

Not many books have been published on the Iran-Iraq conflict, and those that have found their way into print are not always readily available. The following sources deal with this fascinating subject.

The Iran-Iraq War, edited by Tahir-Kheli and Shaheen Ayubi (Praeger, 1983), is thoughtful, balanced, and well structured. Chapters on the Shatt and the historical and religious background of the war are particularly useful.

The Iran-Iraq War, edited by M. S. El Azhary (Canberra, 1984), provides excellent coverage of the long history of the Shatt as well as general information about the war.

The Iran-Iraq War, Islam Embattled, by Stephen R. Grummon (Praeger, 1982), is readable and informative.

Two well-written books about Khomeini's takeover and the radical Islamic sect are *The Reign of the Ayotollah*, by Shaul Bakhash (Basic Books, 1984), and *Iran Since the Revolution*, by Sepehr Zabih (Johns Hopkins University Press, 1982).

An excellent work about the Gulf Region is *Gulf Security into the Eighties: Perceptual and Strategic Dimensions*, edited by Robert G. Darius, John W. Amos II, and

Ralph H. Magnus (Hoover Institution Press, Stanford University, 1984).

The best continuing source of information are current events magazines such as *U.S. News and World Report*, *Time*, and *Newsweek*. Major newspapers such as *The New York Times* also provide daily coverage of the war.

INDEX

ABOUT
THE
AUTHOR

Lisa Mannetti is a Ph.D. candidate
at Fordham University and has
written *Equality* for Franklin Watts.
She resides in Wappingers Falls,
New York.